BREATH ɪɴ EVERY ROOM

BREATH in EVERY ROOM

poems by Tami Haaland

Story Line Press
Ashland, Oregon

Published by Story Line Press, Three Oaks Farm, P.O. Box 1240, Ashland, OR 97520-0055, www.storylinepress.com

This publication was made possible thanks in part to the generous support of the Nicholas Roerich Museum, the Andrew W. Mellon Foundation, the National Endowment for the Arts, and our individual contributors.

Author photo by Robert Ostler
Book design by Lysa McDowell

Library of Congress Cataloging-in-Publication Data
Haaland, Tami, 1960–
        Breath in every room : poems / by Tami Haaland.
            p. cm.
        ISBN 1-58654-016-5
            I. Title.

PS3608.A23 B74 2001
811'.6—dc21   20010497

ACKNOWLEDGMENTS
My thanks to the editors of the following periodicals and anthologies where some of these poems appeared: *Alkali Flats*: "The Dog"; *Calyx*: "Feeding the Sea Girl"; *Clackamas Literary Review*: "After"; *Cowboy Poetry Matters: From Mainstream to Abilene*: "August," "After This"; *5AM*: "Circus," "11:05," "What She Said," "The Idea of Order," "Meeting Valemon"; *Hard Ground II*: "Cleaning the Skin," "The Language of Babies and Birds"; *Intermountain Woman*: "Findings"; *Petroglyph*: "Burying the Placenta," "In July"; *Pif Magazine* (online): "First Trimester," "Goldeye, Vole"; *Rattapallax*: "In the Sky Over Water"; *Ring of Fire: Writers of the Yellowstone Region*: "Cleaning the Office," "In Celebration of Burdock." *Best of Pif Off-line* reprinted "First Trimester"; *Writers Under the Rims* reprinted "11:05" and "August."

My thanks to Jim Peterson, David Lehman, Ed Ochester, Randall Gloege, Donna Davis, and Kathy Woodward who read earlier versions of these poems and offered helpful suggestions. I would like to extend special thanks to Robert McDowell, Lysa McDowell, and Story Line Press for making this book possible.

Finally I would like to thank the AAUW Education Foundation for its financial assistance as I was writing many of these poems.

Contents

I Morning Song

II The Idea of Order

III Findings

IV Not Scientifically Verifiable

For Jim, Philip and Nathan,
and for my mother, Dorothea

1 Morning Song

Cleaning the Skin

It wasn't me who
wanted your head
cut off and buried, but
once it was gone everything
fell into place: my husband
on the phone saying
save the skin; my brother
with knife and pliers; me
with salt and gloves, apologizing,
apologizing, stretching
and pinning you to wood.

Unpinned and dry you come
to my kitchen table. Listen,
old snake, I didn't
want you. Be still, and
let me wash your scales.

August

My cousin was five.
We walked with her to the granaries
to ask the men if they needed food,
to ask if they needed water to drink.
It was harvest. The grass
was dry and crackly. The crop
was pretty good.

When we passed the grease house
we heard the rattle, and
I pulled my cousin's arm,
flipped her belly-down
behind me. She didn't cry,
and my mother told me to run
for the hoe.

She cut three times
to separate the head from
its coiled body, then carried the head
on the blade of the hoe. The mouth
opened and closed, the fangs
bit into air. My mother dug a hole
beside the cottonwood trees
and buried the open mouth there.

She told us to leave that place
alone, told us to watch
so the dogs wouldn't dig.

First Trimester

For three quiet months it's not much more
than a mouse nest behind the pubic bone
so interior no one else can know.
A tiny cataclysm in the body
of the mother, it creates more earwax,
shiny hair, softer flesh, keener smell,
the need for fried eggs in the middle
of the night. It is a transformation
no more noticeable than aphids
colonizing the underside
of sunflower leaves or the soft larvae
of cabbage moths stretching themselves
along the broccoli's interior stems.

In Summer

"Come on," he says
and we go out into the night.
He shines the flashlight on a crumpled leaf,
a paper bag fallen from the sky, a bat
wrapped in parchment wings
on wet grass.

Together we admire tiny fingers,
the longest extending past the tip
of its wing, ears half the size
of its face, ragged teeth
and delicate belly straining
toward flight.

It lifts into the night with no sound
like the bubbles our son set loose
in a whirlwind
that spiraled out of sight.

How Pennies Cry When They Get Lost

My son asks me if I know how, and I don't
because my ears are tuned more to human voice
and washing machines than the sound made
by copper molecules jetting around the head
of Lincoln. You can see, though, how electrons
might spin in invisible tizzy far from proton
and neutron centers, which undoubtedly shiver
at the thought of massive wheels on pavement or
dark nights alone on a dirt road. But I tell him

if the molecules could raise their volume and
if we could listen for the minute cry
of coppery clanging, or even magnify the sound
with some metallic instrument designed for
that purpose alone, well, maybe someone close
to the ground like my son could hear
the tiny vibrations rising dimly in the dark
and in that way a penny could be saved.

When I'm 39

Nathan sings "love is like
a magic penny, hold it tight
and you won't have any."
The teeth he will lose next year
cut into peanut butter and jelly.
He smacks crumbs. It could go on
forever, me smiling across the table
at sticky lips. "Hey Mom," he says,
"you know what I do when
my friends are sad?" He whacks
his fist against his head like
Curly in the Three Stooges.
"Why?" I ask. "Because it
makes them smile," he says.

The Boy's Dream

He crawls into bed late,
afraid to put his head
on the pillow, his dream

still so close. He says
a man wanted olives,
only the olives were really

beetles and the man died.
No, two men ate this fruit
and both died. His face

and body tense
because he likes olives,
especially ripe ones.

Freefall

Sweet boy, in that dream
I was you and felt how you felt
falling through the night sky
with no ground to catch you.
We saw stars, a thick
milky way, and our eyes
squinted to make out letters
strewn across space
in algebraic mystery.
We saw a flash, the head
of medusa, hazy skulls staring
and the sky swallowing them.
We didn't stop falling,
our back aimed for the place
ground was supposed to be,
but we understood, finally,
the faces would not harm us,
and nothing solid
would meet us from below.

Morning Song

The child was bruised one day on the eye,
one day on the bottom. How could this go on?
I told people. "You're dreaming, they said,
calm down." It went like that, another day,
a different bruise and the child
tottering about, little numb thing.

The rescuer in me got ready to pounce.
And if it hadn't been for the robin
on the apple branch I might have
moved the child to a yellow house, bought it
a cat and some horses. The child and I
would have laughed to see the horses
buck and run in summer fallow until dusk.

Monday Afternoon

Philip comes home crabby from school,
turns on the hose, buries it in loose
dirt under the pine trees to make
his own river. Mostly we leave him alone

but after he pokes the banks and dams
the middle, and we agree to turn
down the water so we don't lose it
to the gutter, the littler one and I

step under the pines too, shady place
on a shady day, and break dead branches
that might someday poke an eye.
Before I know it my arms are full

of wood enough to start a fire,
or I could call it waste and walk it
to the backyard dumpster. Night
before last I walked on a mountain

layered in twisted wood, one tree
downed over another, until I reached
two curved pieces connected at top
and bottom with space for me to step

through to the other side. I eased my body
in, set one foot and then the other down.
My relatives came after me then. "Come
back," they yelled, "you need to turn back."

With Fire

He stands on the porch, backlit
by the garage light, drops dried leaves
into the barbecue, stirs with his stick.
Smoke boils around his angular
and delicate six-year old frame.
"Bubble, bubble, toil and trouble,"
he says. "Cauldron brew and cauldron
bubble."

          The leaves ignite.
"Quit," I yell, "or someone will call
the fire department." He faces me
and smoke floats to the alley.
His silhouette moves
to a distant corner of the porch,
returns with a smaller batch of leaves
and drops them on glistening coals.

Scout Meeting at Mayflower Congregational

I step after them toward the open
door of the unlit chapel and stand
at the end of the aisle. Siblings
of scouts, these three and four-year-olds
tip toe into darkness, then halfway
to the altar they spook like horses
in a storm, tossing their heads and
galloping for the doorway's light.

One mother nudges her child away,
another grabs an arm. "Stay
away from there," she says. "A church
is no place to play." I watch the
remaining three, my young son
among them, dancing on toes
toward darkness, whispering into
the center where Jesus waits,
pretending not to notice their approach.

After the Spell

They walk to the side of oncoming cars.
The five-year-old boy, her son, runs
to catch his brother and father. Bright
fair lights, the creak and slam of rides,
pale and grow distant behind them.

She trails after, a gold-starred wand
in her hand, its glittery streamers
dazzling her wrist. By midnight the children
will rest in their own beds. Glass slippers
would break in this graveled parking lot.

At the Game

In the last inning seven-year-olds
swing at air. A cold wind enters
from the northwest like water
through a dam, and five ravens
hover over parents. "Buzzards,"
some say, "hawks." The ravens circle
the field, the park, move higher
and farther south, become
dots against the early evening sun
and then nothing at all.

II   The Idea of Order

Feeding the Sea Girl

She burst from the deep only moments ago
raging about the mess in the kitchen,
laundry stacked against the washer,
the testosterone-fueled super heroes
on afternoon TV. We were surprised

at first by the spiny sea urchins
and anemones caught in her tangled
hair, the bits of kelp and debris hanging
from her eyebrows. This was as angry
as we had ever seen her, and when she

threw the halibut in the living room
and stood over it while it flopped
against chairs and slammed its tail
into the coffee table, we backed
away quietly, spoke in whispers.

She sits in the rocking chair now
eating miniature chocolate bars.
Water has pooled at her feet.
She glares at us and tosses pink
and green candy wrappers to the floor.

The Idea of Order

Sometimes I think that he
thinks that I am not quite
a real woman the way
I can leave beds unmade
and let bills and poems pile up
on the dresser. And sometimes
it annoys me too, like now
when I'm looking for my comb.
So I make the bed and set shoes
in the closet, hang up shirts,
stack books on the desk
and pick up *The Palm*
at the End of the Mind, dropped
beside menstrual pads and
earrings and the wildflowers
I put in a cup. And beneath
the book, I find the comb.

Lipstick

I wonder how they do it, those women
who can slip lipstick over lips without
looking, after they've finished a meal
or when they ride in cars. Satin Claret
or Plum or Twig or Pecan. I can't stay
inside the lines, late comer to lipstick
that I am, and sometimes get messy
even in front of a mirror. But these
women know where lips end and plain
skin begins, probably know how to put
their hair in a knot with a single pin.

In the Afternoon

You should have a wild
rose in your mouth, he said,
and I pulled the pen
from my teeth. Life is
like that, I said. Just
when you think you
should be dancing
it occurs to you
the kitchen sink still
needs to be cleaned and
you go after it with
vinegar and soda thinking
you'll be satisfied
to make it sparkle.

Cleaning the Office

Essays and handouts go into files.
I toss memos into the recycling, old mail
into the trash, wipe down the desktop,
dust off the shelves, and the office
is clean except that poems
scatter around the computer,
chocolate smears the keyboard,
and this note written on birch bark, found
in the pages of a secondhand book,
leans against the calendar:
Sweet Sara, tonight we sleep
under the full moon, maybe hear wolves,
breathe the scent of fir and pine.
You would like it here Sara. Bear grass
grows along the mountain, paintbrush
and gentian stretch up from the creek,
sparks from the fire swirl
and dissolve under stars.

Before the Work Was Done

She hardly looked at the bergamot
and black-eyed Susan blooming
around angelica which bloomed
too beneath cottonwood
and chokecherry that ventured
up through granite along the west
bank of the river. But after she made
herself look, the plate-sized leaves
of burdock were all she saw
and the stalks narrowing to flowers
that would turn to rusty burrs,
cling to deer and elk, gray
and wither, their seeds spilled.
She walked out to run fingertips
over deep-veined leaves, patterns
of ridges and soft down, like hands,
she thought, clean and cold.

Slicing an Egg

Make every word count, I say
to my students the way
my mother said make every step
count in the kitchen. Still I bumble
after so many years, forget
to bring salt to the table,
return twice for the gallon
of milk. Today, I hold a boiled
egg in my palm, slice it
into salad. I nick the fleshy underside
of a finger and remember her
with a towel around her hand
stirring gravy and hauling
dinner to the field before
she drove to town for stitches.

After

We stand at the washing machine picking
straw from our son's new sweater
after he has tripped in a pumpkin patch
and run through amaranth with his
second grade friends. Our fingers
ease slivers from the fibers, back
then front, stomach, shoulders,
arms, after a morning of angry
glares, an afternoon of looking
away then opening to talk about
weather and people we know.
Our fingers examine this fabric for
odd texture, the barbs buried deep.

Breath in Every Room

First came the usual ones, soft
infants who pressed their toes
against her nightgown, curled

into her breast, then larger ones,
rambunctious in their lightest
sleeping. From under the bed

some grabbed her ankles—not
always—and some climbed down
from curtains where dust

gathered, whispered over
the pillow and knotted
her hair. In the dark hallway

they brushed fingertips against
her shoulders then disappeared
if the light came on.

The tiny ones behind
her eyes almost never
came out, though she could

see them in the dark when
the children were still
in their own beds and she lay

awake to the sounds of breath
in every room, watching
their faces dissolve.

Fever

In the kitchen, forehead resting on palms,
I focus on the mottled 70s linoleum
beneath my chair, where I see faces
of old men with beards and long
noses and disproportionate arms, who
might be Freud or a man by the sea
with jagged teeth and bent jaw.
And I don't mind finding them
in the heat and chill of this room.

There were faces, too, in the hilly
metal seat backs when I was a girl
riding home on the school bus—
a dwarf sometimes with pointed cap,
sometimes whole colonies and roads
that shifted into new scenes
when the bus lurched over patches
of gravel.

           But when the older boy
reached for my legs as I lay on
the green vinyl bench, I pressed
myself against the wall of the bus
and became the sweet girl who sat
so nicely in her seat, who stared
at dry grass in the roadside
and the distance we had to go.

July 3

Red-tailed hawks circle the sun and
light trickles through their feather tips.
Father and sons light firecrackers
and smoke bombs in the bulldozed edge
of a road. Beyond, a hill lifts into sandstone
overhang, scrubby fir, and the calls of
meadowlarks, chickadees and flickers.
"Come with me," I say to my young son,
but he won't go far from the others.

Crackling and flames spread near the roots
of a juniper. "A fire," I say, "you started a fire."
"Don't stand there," he says, and
I jump the trickle of creek between us,
throw shale on the circle of flames.
He covers it with mud, then lights another fuse.
At dinner, they talk of twenty-twos
and shot guns, pheasant hunting and
the gutting of deer. Our sons' hair is cut
close to their heads, nothing to tousle.

When he was ten my brother shot a sparrow
out of our biggest cottonwood. We circled
the fallen bird, my cousins and brother
and I, watched those last breaths, and
my brother scooped the bird into his hand.
I'm looking for the horse to set loose
like the girl in that Alice Munro story,
send it through the gate though
the father will catch it anyway.

The Dog

I hated seeing her
split like a shot deer, burst
from her skin because a truck shifted down
too late. I heard the shift
walking from the wheat to the house
thinking a month had passed
since the moon was big and we came home
facing it late one night.

We squatted to touch her head,
her hips, the rest sprawled, a steamy
sculpture, water falling from rock, her blood
still draining on harvest dust.

We dug near the wild plums
to ground so hard we had to beat
each piece with iron
and carried her in a green spread,
turned red, to a hole four feet deep.

The neighbors gathered under the yard light
to talk of broken wrenches,
headers run into rock,
how soon they would finish,
how much they would make,
while we covered her,
pushed the dirt down hard
in the dark.

In the morning
I scraped her liver into weeds
off the road, covered blood
to disappoint the flies.

III   Findings

What Circles in the Dark

It moves along the fence, a squeak,
a click of tongue and teeth, passing
too quickly for anything
but warm blood. The night sky
is hazy, the moon not up, the porch
too distant to light this place.
I pull my toes into sandals,
hear it slide from chain link then
click its teeth in front of me.

I stomp my foot.
                        It stops
then speaks again in tongue
and teeth sounds, closer, its
eyes undaunted.

                        I bolt
for the back door, over toys,
past wet grass, bounding
high and quick, the image
of teeth on my heels.

After This

The rain came though we didn't
smell it coming on the wind
because of the smoke. The forests
were burning, there were bright
sunsets in the west but that's summer—
if not lightning then some

nut with a match, some camper
who hacks at lodgepole until it
drips sap, then tosses cans
under the picnic table and lets
the campfire smolder. We might
not have noticed at all

because of the fires but
the clouds settled in over smoke
and the rain rattled the fiberglass
roof of the shed and the children
danced and after this,
we could not leave.

In July

I ran and scared the spider
who ran for the window
and the apple branches beyond.
I slowed down, so did she.

I stopped, bent to look, smiled.
She turned, lowered her back legs,
pushed up on her two front legs
until one dangled. Her flat blue eyes

and my two eyes met somewhere
between faucet and shower curtain
when the first apples were falling
and the rain was gathering

above the house. She licked
her legs, rubbed them against
her face. I washed my hands,
combed and smoothed my hair.

The Garden

One day, my mother showed me
how to peel a squash blossom
from its stamen and touch it
to the interior of the female
flower so flecks of pollen stay
in the pale yellow crevice.

A little girl, she asked her mother
why seeds grew when you planted them.
Didn't dead people get buried too?

I lifted the vine, brought half
a dozen strawberries to light and
shook away the thin yellow spider
on my palm. I wanted it back then,
and my fingers sifted through leaves,
looking for what was gone.

Kelp

Reconstituted, dry stick turned to branches,
see-through green with specks, backbone

with fronds, waistband of a skirt and
below it, gathered silk. See how fingers

block light? Someone facing you could see
your lips and chin pressed to the other side.

Swirled pieces spin in current the way
you wish you could twirl and bend. Smell

sand dollars and stones on a beach, taste
salt on your lips, your own thin piece of sea.

In Celebration of Burdock

Stretching up through crags
along the Stillwater, among chokecherries
or in rows in my mother's garden
it grows showy as any dahlia or iris,
persistent as prickly pear.

On the stone covered sandbar
along Rock Creek one summer
I found its purple blossoms
just opening, then dreamed about it
in February, how its roots felt
their way through rocks to the wet
sand below and the clay below that,
how its leaves extended from its center
toward cottonwoods that reflected
and filtered the sun, toward potentilla
and plantain, and the smell
of mossy water slipping past.

Water

The steam rising from your elevated
knee will evaporate when the bath water drains.
Later those same cycling molecules
might filter past your throat
into the slick folds of your stomach,
into the tiny villi of your small intestine,
rinsing permeable layers of cells, bathing
your resident bacteria, passing
into the deep red of your kidneys, then
flowing down the drain to the river,
where a deer will lap the water you
have been drinking, and the wiry haired
muskrat will slip through it, gills will
open and close around it, Canadian geese
will wet their feathers, and the rock worm
will lie in the shallows waiting
for the emergence of wings.

Capture

This weekend it was snakes from the park.
The boys found a hole close to the pond
and their fingers pulled out garter snakes.
When the boys carried them past balsamroot
and chokecherries, the snakes
wrapped themselves around wrists,
their heads lying on forearms
or aimed forward into the path, dainty
black-tipped tongues flicking in smells.

Once it was a dragonfly in the front yard.
Its wings moved only a fraction, not strong
enough to lift it off cement. We scooped it
onto a plate, put it under the pine trees,
and when the cats got too close,
placed it in the center of the kitchen table.
We gave it green grass, drops of water,
created a small habitat on plastic.
At dinner its tail aimed at the ceiling
then fell limp and dull on the grass.

Last spring we caught frogs
in a water-filled gravel bed,
put them in a bucket in the backyard,
built guards against the cats.
We listened to their love songs at night,
found them mating in the morning
and escaping by noon.
Today over afternoon ice cream,
our son tells us that he caught a slug once
and when no one was looking
he tore its body open with his fingers
to discover its tiny heart.

Black Widow

Her long hind legs truss up the cricket
like a cowboy tying a calf
at the rodeo, and she leaves it,
heads to a far corner
of the canning jar, then attacks
and bites until the life is gone.

The boys try to understand
why she mates then kills
and eats the male.
The neighbor girl tells us
anti-venom will work only once.

She rests on her web
near the floor of her jar.
Below, a husk of centipede
hangs on its back, its head
tipped. I stand on a chair,
wash the window above her,
imagine slipping and
fumbling, the crash of jar.

Living in Jars

Imagine how you would feel
walking along your own
dependable trail in the forest
and a giant, hairy topped, two-legged
thing screams for his mother
to get a jar because he thinks
you must be poisonous, screams again
because he's never seen one of you
before. He's young and you know
by your sudden indigestion
that he may be dangerous
so in your quiet way,
you slide your six legs farther
into dried grass, drag your exposed
abdomen along. And in your fright,
you step into the dead
end of his hand or his mother's
sweater and find yourself jostled
into a clear thing, abdomen over
head over hairy back heels.
You find yourself settled
on the bottom, bounced along the trail,
exposed to children's faces, your
tiny antennae ringing with their
high-pitched voices, and you
end up sitting in the clear thing,
in a quiet corner of a room,
hoping that the large-eyed children
will remember your food.

Durable Placement

Ants outnumber people probably
20,000 to one. In a city of, say,
100,000 there might be
two billion ants, mostly
female, hilling their way
along sidewalks, tunneling
through grass roots, creeping
past dried caulk into bathrooms.
Some cultivate fungus along
musty walls, the outgrowth
of a pasty white flake carried
to the colony on the belly
of the queen. Some turn
themselves into storage jugs,
hang by their back legs
in a cavern, their gullets
filled with honey taken
from the gall of a wasp.

In our yard, ants
tap feet over buds
to coax the petals of peony
and yucca into light, or
herd aphids on honeysuckle,
spit bugs on sunflowers.
The most adventurous explore
compost piles and tunnel
cities into the underside
of yarrow.

They live
under prairie grass
between my mother's mailbox
and her house, generations
descended from relatives
who crawled beneath bison
or from distant relatives who
lived on the edge of a receding
Cretaceous sea. If human life
were gone they would continue
to thread their way deeper
into clay, uncovering
the reason for the next
curve, testing grains
for durable placement.

Worms

When we were five and six my cousins
and I caught caterpillars in the firebush,
put them in a clear jar and filled it
with Lysol and hair spray.

On the cement one summer
I squashed a green caterpillar
under my bare foot and screamed
at the thought of its explosion.

I bit into a walnut, felt a tug,
pulled against it then let the walnut
fall from my mouth. The worm escaped
onto the counter and I ran to the bedroom
to shake the idea away.

At 3 a.m. one summer I walked out
under the full moon, felt wet membranes
sliding along the arches of my feet, the slick
night crawlers rising between toes.

My son tried to put a caterpillar
in my hand. It won't hurt you, he said.

One day we watched a single tent worm
crawling toward us, reaching for a body
or tree to climb on, lifting its blind head
left, then center, then right, like an infant
looking for a nipple in the dark.

Swallowtail

No longer caterpillars
stuffing ourselves and growing rotund,
vaguely happy not to be squashed
by tricycle tires or snapped
into the black mouth
of a grackle, now our fat bodies
have become wingspan
and brilliance, our edges,
curved into lace. We slip
tongues into flowers,
feed upon carcasses and
dance up the linden tree
past flies and robins, our
yellow and black down reflected
in the moisture of eyes.

Chance

You might find sprouted seeds
in January under snow, or the abdomen
of a hornet on the bedroom
floor, hair lining its hard curves.
Maybe you find a pea clam
in the opening of a snail shell,
or a wasp reaching for the shell's
dried interior with its tendriled
feet and pincered mouth. A crow
could bury a chicken bone
in the branches of a spruce and
you might think it's a lucky day.

Just imagine what happens
among the things you can't see,
the dust mites, for instance,
on your desk or this page,
nibbling your shed skin.
If only you could see microbes,
the odd collision and accidental
turning and tripping, one mixing itself
with another and multiplying wildly
because it can. Breathe in now,
imagine the raucous turning
in the world of your lungs,
the frantic escape into
blood or air, and then
the settling in, the celebration.

Experiment

Let's begin with the mouse, small gray carcass
the cat left on the walk. Enter wasps, aggressive
according to season. It's morning, mid-August.

They begin with the jelly eye, eat to
bone socket, then go for the hollow of neck,
snip through fur to sinewy meat, trim

to vertebrae, tunnel under collar bone, scissor
through skin and gorge on dark viscera.
Their tiny feet step inside to outside, outside to in

until each white sliver of rib brightens in the sun.
The skull shines as they trim away tendons, the muscles
of cheek and jaw, then gnaw to the backbone

and into the pelvis, their wings tossing them
sometimes to flight, sheer joy of the feast
in a dry season, until they descend again.

Findings

Found what I think are the breast feathers
of a flicker lying in the melting snow
in front of the house. Found a crow feather
in Bozeman one spring and have kept it
in a vase on top of the dresser. Yarrow grows
where my son planted a root last summer,
and hyssop seeds have sprouted
with the wildflowers. Found spearmint
growing under the outside faucet
and tiny blue snails in the fallen apples
and black and white hornets stumbling drunk
around the rotting apples in August. The columbine
had eight inches of new growth in January,
and two summers ago found a red-shafted flicker
lying in the alley behind my house
with grass in its throat and wasps
crawling in and out of its mouth.
Its wing feathers were dazzling
and I took them, buried its body
in tall weeds, saved the feathers
in checkbook boxes in the dresser
beside a Norwegian pewter cake server,
a twenty dollar bill, some old ribbons
and a flat rock from the Marias.
His mate remained in the neighborhood until fall,
and this February a pair of flickers returned
to eat last year's sunflower seeds
at the side of the garage.
One spring, hundreds of crows filled a single tree,

their black wings shifting against dense bodies
and air, their voices calling across leaves
then reeling into space.
Saw flickers in the park last spring,
a male calling with such racket
my son covered his ears, and
from across the park, through twigs
and leaves pushing out from resinous shells,
a female approached, blended into bark
and clouds, and for an instant, opened to the sound.

IV   Not Scientifically Verifiable

Lecture

"For me, the spirit world is very real."
She stands at the podium looking
at rows of students above her.
"Freed from space and time it might
exist here at this moment, only
we can't see it. Let's say it does."

Someone heckles from the back
"realism or nothing" and
Van Gogh winks at Joyce whose eyes
glimmer over the woman's shoulder.
"I knew someone like that," Van Gogh says.
"Think of the damage he might do among

the living." The room begins to feel warm.
"Don't worry, my dear," says George Eliot.
"Remember the squirrel's heartbeat?"
What am I doing? she asks herself. *Believe,
fine, but why announce?* "Yes, I see your point,"
she says to the man, whom Van Gogh

is painting into a spiral of sun, "but how
can you be so sure realism is the way
to go?" she says. "Think of . . ."
"Me!" Van Gogh shouts, "Me, Me!"
"Think of . . . oh, you know, the man
who painted sunflowers," and Van Gogh

slings red ochre at the wall behind her.
"Or think of Roethke talking with
plants," she says. "Yes, yes, they could
hear me," says Roethke, "but you should have
heard what they said." Van Gogh
swirls night and stars onto the chalk board

and Joyce joins Roethke mid-aisle where
they mime Book I of *Paradise Lost*, lolling
about the floor like devils. Milton
scowls from the rafters, though he, too,
agrees about realism and says so
to Dizzy Gillespie who blows his trumpet

over all their heads. Flood gates
appear on the horizon and Eliot gazes
at the scene near the speaker
who moves on to her next point,
which has nothing to do with realism,
which was beside the point anyway.

In the Beginning

To look at us, you might not think
we came from ice. The cow, Audumla,
congealed from river water: first

liquid coursing, then collecting
and the round cow stepping onto
the bank. She found the ice, planted

her feet, solid now, against the edge
of the glacier and began to lick—
heat of her grainy tissue against cold—

lick and lick until hair caught
the buds of her tongue, and below it,
the slick forehead of our ancestor.

Pliable under her warmth, nose,
lips, and chin loosened, eyelids
lifted. Finally, the entire ancestor, upright,

roared below the heated breath of the cow.
After that we came from him, somehow,
unsure of our mother. Standing on

the glacier top, we watch Audumla
dissolve its edge below us. Surely
something comes next.

On the Blackfoot

The ice, he yelled, look
at the ice and we left
our papers and pens and ran
for our coats, then down
the wooden stairs and across
the yard into willows
and over rocks, the still
cool air on our faces, to stand
at the edge and watch
the wild flash of water, cracks
giving way to current, chunks
heaving one over the other,
collecting, then pushing through.

Circus

The fleshy bears walk upright, muzzled and
leashed as if to catch a scent, then kiss

their trainers. The grizzly jumps bright hurdles,
plants haunches on metal bleachers and twitches

her foot, her snout down. My heart hangs low—
what else can it do? My fingers want to bury

their tips in her chest. And the spirit? I think it calls
up, up, to the heart, and to the fingers, *yes.*

Stories

Woman goes to the forest and meets
bear, who invites her to pick berries
deeper in, where she can see light play
against leaves. She's fascinated
at this upright bear, and she can't
help but think the berries look better
under those farther trees. So she takes
her basket, follows bear, picks berries
while he watches.

           Or maybe she has
a dream before she ever goes
into the forest. She dreams of a wreath
and the next day here comes bear
tossing it around. She wants it so badly she
walks right up to him, taps him on his hairy belly.

One way or another, she goes with him.
By the time she sees how the story
is walking through her, she smells salmon
on the wind, knows how roots
trail through loam. In time she abandons
the basket or wreath and begins
to understand the odd shape
of her hands, lined and calloused,
digging in forest dirt.

Meeting Valemon

I dreamed the circle of flowers first,
hyacinth and heather wound
into clematis, and in the morning
life without it was impossible.

Then he walked into the yard,
this talking bear,
tossing the wreath, teasing.
I asked if I could have it, felt

his breath on my forehead, sweet
like berries. And he gave it to me,
then said I must leave with him
in three days or he would take it back.

My father called in his army.
Big men lined the castle wall, shot
their arrows, threw their spears—
nothing could touch him. My sisters

went out but he turned
them away, wanted only me
and I wanted to go.
I ride on his back now,

holding long white hair
that springs from his shoulders,
soft hair, smelling of the forest
we are about to enter.

Goldeye, Vole

I say sweep of prairie
or curve or sandstone,

but it doesn't come close
to this language of dry wind

and deer prints, blue racer
and sage, its punctuation

white quartz and bone.
I learned mounds of

mayflowers, needle grass
on ankles, the occasional

sweet pea before I knew
words like perspective or

travesty or the permanence
of loss. My tongue spoke

obsidian, red agate,
arrowhead. I stepped

through tipi rings, leaped
buffalo grass and puff ball

to petrified clam.
Jawbone of fox, flint,

blue lichen, gayfeather,
goldeye, vole—speak to me

my prairie darling, sing me
that song you know.

Love Song

Maybe it's a thread, no color or many, or an old-
fashioned dance on a wooden floor with fiddlers
in the corner. Maybe it's a prayer in Persian or
a pipe ceremony in Lapwai, or you spinning
on the grass, twirling and falling to watch sky
turn to the tune of your eyes. The body thinks
it's a rope to climb on, wrap between legs on its
way to the ceiling. But even that ends in separation.
I sign my letters love, meaning, I give you
my love, and love me, please. You are so far away
and here I am, playing with knotted strings.

Play

Give the body heat and it will
adjust, feel a chill. Another piece
of chocolate please, more sun,
the last bite of scallops. Maybe
a walk, it says, in the coulee
where the hawk flies. And
more love, says the heart.
It chases its tail, can't figure
what it's after. Mornings,
when I sit to pray, the dog
puts her paws in my lap,
licks my knuckles. I don't
know why she comes to play
whenever I close my eyes.

What She Said

27, 34, 46, he don't know much,
she said, God don't know much
and we need to ask him
for a lot of help, we need help,
we need to listen, oh listen,
I listen here and over here
and over here, we need help.

She pulled tissues
from the box, tossed them
to the air. Bye bye,
she said, I want
to go, I don't want,
I think, oh tilly, oh pilly,
name oh name.

She leaned forward
and back. Oh nobody
realizes, she said,
you don't understand, I want
to go to bed, I don't want
to go to bed.

The Language of Babies and Birds

My hand runs down your arm,
along parchment skin speckled
like the eggs of songbirds,
and my fingers touch delicate folds
above the inside of your elbow
crinkled like the fine white fabric
of a skirt gathered to its waistband.

In the course of this day your upper lip
has disappeared into the darkness
of your mouth where ridges of skin
converge and drops of raspberry
morphine dry and remain. Your feet,
swollen for two weeks now, have become
the dark purple base of canyon walls

that curve above them, that seep
down into amber blisters
on toes. And today you leave
words behind and begin speaking
in musical runs, in two-tone
descensions from on high,
in the language of babies and birds.

We sit holding hands.
I hum to you the spring call
of the black-capped chickadee, second
and tonic, the song
you have chosen, and you echo
my hum from some distant place
as we sing our way toward dusk.

That Light

Afterwards came the dream
about the dry sac. I poured
oil over it and the baby
swelled into infant shape. Its fingers
extended from open palms, the soft
skin of its head reflected the lamp,
and I felt like clapping and
shouting, it was so much more
than dead cells. The next day
I closed my eyes and wrapped
that dream baby in flannel.
For whole minutes I held it
in my arms and loved it.

Then I stepped through a doorway
into a place with wooden floors,
white walls and sunlight, where
an old woman waited in a rocker.
I placed the child in her arms and
unraveled myself. She took the baby,
but did not look up, and I turned
and walked away from that light.

Burying the Placenta

Frozen for sixteen weeks
it comes out
of its bowl into my hands,
and I understand now
how the membranes spiraled
from the base of the cord
to carry my son.

I kneel over this knee-deep hole
near the comfrey, let it
slip from my hands, clotty
and whole, as beautiful
as frog's eggs at the river's
edge or red clay
washed down from a cliff.

My hands push dirt,
a night crawler falls in
and my fingers smooth the soil.
I sprinkle sage on wet
ground, feel my heart pound
the finality of the thing.

Sweet Grass Hills

Through our north living room window
you could see rock rising above trees
on the center mountain. We had
pictures of a picnic: my dad,
his parents, the kids from church—
Lutherans from out North and
the green willows beside the creek.

He walked to a cave with his friends
that day, but it was so long ago, he said
he couldn't remember the way back.

My mother and I took my small son
across dirt roads to these hills that
rise from prairie. We found
sage scattered along the ground,
tobacco ties in trees. I left
my mother and son resting near rock,
ran down a trail and wanted to
continue around every next curve.

One night I saw movement on
the center mountain, hills turned
into women sitting knee to knee
in a circle, their torsos and long
hair rising, falling, swaying to
the pulse of some invisible drum.

A Short History of Giants

He wasn't big at first
but when he moved into one
scene and then another

he had the chance
to love—nothing sexy—
just get along, let his

heart open like a complete moon
in a clear sky until whatever
contained him fell away and

he grew taller and wider.
Then he found himself
in some other scene,

changed scenes seven times
to be exact, until
he grew to nine or ten feet tall

with shoulders wide enough
to bear the height. After that
he left the story, and I imagine

he's out there still, probably
invisible by now, too big
for human eyes to see.

Fragments

In a glass case near the science room
the head of homo habilis inhabits a shelf, blue
clay matching features to fragments of bone,
rounding hollows that eyes would have filled.

A small man steps into the room; his voice
fills the space around homo habilis, whose
blue clay face refuses change. He sees hollow
bones, imagines the heart pumping the spirit awake.

I wake to a clatter: fragments of song last
night in a room with blue lights in the corners
and a checkered floor. It could have been
the far edges of an undercut cave, dark

blue ashes of a fire where homo habilis came in
with skins, left fragments of supper bones, the cave
a hollow room. The floor filled with beating hearts last
night, bone and song pieced together for the dance.

Chocolate

My friend brings me chocolate macadamia nut whales
from Hawaii, mother whale swimming with baby
under her fin, long mouth, dot of an eye. I tell her

we bought my mother frilly hearts filled with chocolate
for Valentine's day, candies I would bite into and put
back until I found a caramel to melt on my tongue.

I wanted to grow up, I tell her, so I could have
my own pretty heart, and I'm still waiting. My friend
had a friend who spent her whole allowance on

chocolate covered cherries for a girl she liked. They
went to a ballgame together and the girl went off
with someone else. There she was, my friend's friend,

those chocolate covered cherries mashed and
gooey in the pocket of her coat. Girls are like that,
we say. My whale, near a shipwreck of paper

on the ocean of my desk, sends its sugary scent
to me on waves, says maybe we could swim when
this work is done. There are worlds we need to see.

Not Scientifically Verifiable

What if I walk around the corner and
fish swim into my mind, and when a man
I don't know walks past me the thought
leaps into his mind and later he mentions
to his wife that he would like to have fish
and so she goes out to get some, since
he asked, and the word escapes from her
thoughts into the mind of the woman
in aisle three who passes it to the checker
and so on.

Only, what if I am really
thinking of your breath on my neck, my
fingers on your shoulders, your palm on
the curve of my waist. We could explain
how these thoughts leap from one mind
to another with words like pheromone or
hormone. It's harder to say why fish might
take this course except they have been
known to swim upstream five hundred miles,
as you or I might, if only for a slim chance.

In the Sky over Water

She is a thin, clear note
in the sky over water.

Until the song is through,
she is sound, not flesh.

It would be so easy to arrive,
to become the last note and

then the echo before silence,
but she wants to be what lasts

and does not last, not the last
note but the one before.

11:05

This is my tired poem when the ash
leaves turn and willows by the river
sift theirs to the ground; this is my
turning in poem, my singing poem
about the dog curled into old blankets
and cats rattling dishes in the sink.
This is for sleep, for you who have
begun to sink into the deep water
of dreams where I am swimming
to meet you in tall weeds and we
wait for the next big fish. This is my
swimming poem when we rise
to its belly, hold to its spiked fins and
follow it into the open waters of this lake.

Notes

"July 3":
The Alice Munro story is "Boys and Girls."

"Lecture":
The "squirrel's heart beat" is taken from George Eliot's novel, *Middlemarch*. "If we had a keen vision and feeling of all ordinary human life, it would be like hearing the grass grow and the squirrel's heart beat, and we should die of that roar which lies on the other side of silence" (Chapter 20).

"In the Beginning":
This poem is a retelling of a Norse creation myth in which a female cow brings the primordial ancestor, Buri, from the ice. Odin, Vili and Ve, the "we" of the poem, are Buri's grandsons, though I've adapted the story to make it appear as if they are his sons. In the original, his son, Bor, came into being without a mother.

"Goldeye, Vole":
Goldeye is a colloquial name for a fish in the Marias River drainage of Montana.

"Love Song":
Lapwai is a town on the Nez Pierce Reservation in Idaho.

"Fragments":
Homo Habilis, the earliest human species, lived between 2.2 and 1.6 million years ago in east Africa and was thought to be the first fire builder and maker of tools.